THE *featured* Flutist

Made Easy!

T0061308

FREE hints and tips downloadable
to your computer.
Visit: www.featuredseries.com
Registration is free and easy.
Your registration code is: TF367

Boston Music Company
part of The Music Sales Group
New York/Los Angeles/Nashville/London/Berlin/Copenhagen/Madrid/Paris/Sydney/Tokyo

Published by
Boston Music Company

Exclusive Distributors:
Music Sales Corporation
257 Park Avenue South, New York, NY 10010 USA

Music Sales Limited
14-15 Berners Street, London W1T 3LJ England

Music Sales Pty. Limited
120 Rothschild Street, Rosebery, Sydney, NSW 2018, Australia

Order No. BMC-11957
ISBN 0-8256-3476-8

Translated & edited by Rebecca Taylor.

Printed in the United States of America by
Vicks Lithograph and Printing Corporation

Your Guarantee of Quality:
As publishers, we strive to produce every book
to the highest commercial standards.

The book has been carefully designed to minimize awkward page turns
and to make playing from it a real pleasure. Particular care has been given
to specifying acid-free, neutral-sized paper made from pulps
which have not been elemental chlorine bleached.

This pulp is from farmed sustainable forests and
was produced with special regard for the environment.

Throughout, the printing and binding have been planned
to ensure a sturdy, attractive publication which should give
years of enjoyment.

If your copy fails to meet our high standards, please inform us
and we will gladly replace it.

www.musicsales.com

Scherzino

Music by Joachim Andersen

Minuet

Music by Johann Sebastian Bach

Gavotte

Music by Johann Sebastian Bach

Minuet In G

Music by Ludwig van Beethoven

Habañera

Music by Georges Bizet

Concerto In D

Music by Luigi Boccherini

Waltz

Music by Johannes Brahms

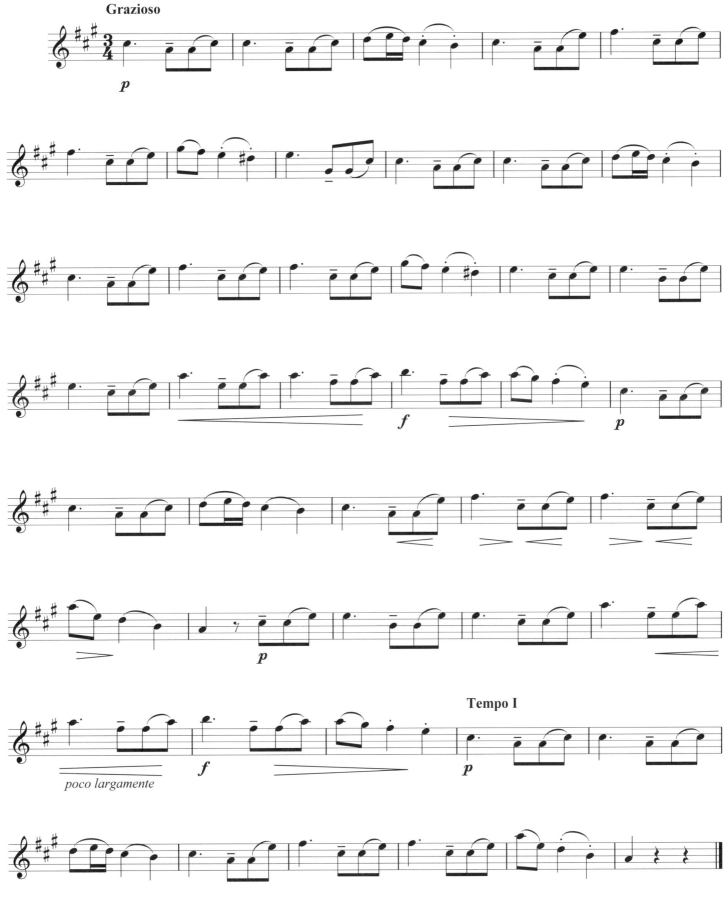

Ah! So Pure

Music by Friedrich von Flotow

Solveig's Song

Music by Edvard Grieg

Andante con moto

Sonata No.2
(Second Movement: Andante)

Music by George Frederic Handel

Sarabande

Music by George Frederic Handel

Arioso

Music by George Frederic Handel

Cradle Song

Music by Miska Hauser

Andante tranquillo

Serenade

Music by Joseph Haydn

Trio No.4

Music by Joseph Haydn

On Wings Of Song

Music by Felix Mendelssohn

Barcarolle

Music by Jacques Offenbach

Skater's Waltz

Music by Emile Waldteufel

CD Track Listing

1. **Scherzino**
   (Andersen)

2. **Minuet**
   (Bach)

3. **Gavotte**
   (Bach)

4. **Minuet In G**
   (Beethoven)

5. **Habañera**
   (Bizet)

6. **Concerto In D**
   (Boccherini)

7. **Waltz**
   (Brahms)

8. **Ah! So Pure**
   (Flotow)

9. **Solveig's Song**
   (Grieg)

10. **Sonata No.2**
    (Second Movement: Andante)
    (Handel)

11. **Sarabande**
    (Handel)

12. **Arioso**
    (Handel)

13. **Cradle Song**
    (Hauser)

14. **Serenade**
    (Haydn)

15. **Trio No.4**
    (Haydn)

16. **On Wings Of Song**
    (Mendelssohn)

17. **Barcarolle**
    (Offenbach)

18. **Skater's Waltz**
    (Waldteufel)